A Buzzing Problem

Rosina Thompson
Art by Gemma Hastilow

Literacy Consultants
David Booth • Kathleen Corrigan

Contents

Chapter 1

Becoming Queen

The hive was always a busy place, with bees coming and going from sunrise until sunset. But today was different. It seemed even busier than usual. Queen Matilda's reign was over, and all the bees were busy cleaning the hive. They were getting it ready for the new queen.

Queen Beth always knew that this day would come. She was raised to take over when Queen Matilda's time was done.

Clara, a nurse bee, buzzed around the queen and said, "Beth, can you believe it? You are now the queen!"

"I know, Clara. But I am not sure that I am ready," said Beth.

Clara stopped buzzing and sat next to Beth. The young worker bee said to Beth, "You will be a great queen. You were chosen when you were just a larva. I personally fed you royal jelly your entire life so that you would grow up to be a queen."

Beth looked at Clara and gave her a hug. "Thanks, Clara. You always know just what to say. I will miss spending time with you and the other nurse bees."

"We will miss you too! Please visit if you get the chance," begged Clara.

"I hope I can," replied Beth.

A group of attendants came to escort Queen Beth to her new quarters. She looked back at Clara and waved as she was swept away.

The next day was just as busy. The worker bees all helped keep the hive running smoothly. The young worker bees — nurse bees — were feeding the larvae. Other worker bees were doing other tasks. Some were cleaning the cells and getting them ready for nectar and pollen. Others were busy repairing and building the honeycomb. Still others were keeping everyone cool by fanning their wings. The guards were on the lookout, making sure that no unwanted insects got into the hive. Older worker bees had left the hive to search for flowers to collect nectar and pollen. The male bees, called drones, were the only ones who were not hard at work.

Chapter 2

A Buzzing Problem

Queen Beth was getting familiar with her new duties. Karina was an older worker bee. She had been busy foraging all week and had realized something strange. That morning, Karina stayed behind to consult with Queen Beth instead of leaving the hive to forage.

Karina explained to Beth that lately the foragers had been struggling to get back before sunset. They were having to travel very far from the hive to find sources of pollen and nectar.

"Why are the foragers having to go so far?" asked Beth. Knowing that foragers were capable of traveling as far as six miles in a day, Beth added, "Isn't there food within six miles of the hive?"

"In some cases the foragers must fly even farther away to find the resources we need. Some foragers don't make it back before sunset," replied Karina.

Queen Beth looked puzzled. "What is happening to all the gardens and fields?" she asked.

"They are being replaced!" exclaimed Karina. "Humans are destroying gardens and fields to build houses. And some farmers use poisonous chemicals on their plants. Those chemicals are harmful to bees."

"What can we do?" asked Beth. She was really worried about her hive and her foragers.

"I do not know," said Karina, buzzing anxiously.

Queen Beth looked frustrated. "Some humans do not realize that a third of their food depends on pollination. They will not be able to grow as much food if the foragers do not help pollinate their plants."

Beth spent a sleepless night trying to figure out a way to save her hive. She needed a solution that would keep her hive safe and healthy.

The next morning, Beth went around the hive in search of Clara. Clara always knew what to do.

Clara was surprised to see Beth. "What are you doing here, Beth? Or should I say, Your Majesty."

Beth smiled, "Oh, Clara! I am still just Beth. I wanted to get your thoughts on something."

"Whatever you need!" responded Clara, eager to help Beth with anything she could.

"I need some ideas on how to fix a very big problem," said Beth. "The gardens and fields where we get our nectar and pollen are being destroyed. The resources we need are too far away. What can we do?"

"Easy," said Clara with a smile. "We bring the gardens and fields to us," she said jokingly.

Queen Beth laughed. "How do we do that?"

Then she stopped laughing and with an excited buzz, she threw her arms around Clara. "I've got it!" she shouted as she quickly flew away, leaving a puzzled-looking Clara behind.

Queen Beth rushed back to her quarters and shouted for Karina. "Karina, how far away is the closest garden or field that has the right plants for us to collect nectar and pollen?"

"It is the distance of a full day's flight," answered Karina.

"Are there any foragers that are capable of flying there and back?" inquired Beth.

"I can think of some that would be able to make it, although not all bees could make the trip in a single day."

"Please bring them to me."

"Yes, right away, Your Majesty," Karina said.

Within an hour, Queen Beth had ten worker bees buzzing in front of her.

Chapter 3

The Search Party

Beth looked at each forager with a very serious expression on her face. "I have a very important mission for you all. It will be dangerous, but our very existence relies on your abilities. Are you willing to take on such a task?"

All ten foragers looked at Beth with an equally serious expression on their faces. "Yes, Your Majesty!" they all shouted.

Queen Beth very carefully explained her plan, and the foragers quickly left to begin their dangerous mission.

After the foragers had left, Queen Beth looked at Karina. "Did I do the right thing?"

"You did the only thing that will save this hive," Karina replied.

Clara came around the corner, saying, "Queen Beth, you flew off before you could tell me what you were so excited about! Did you come up with a solution to the problem?"

Beth turned to Clara with an apology. "Sorry, Clara. I was in a hurry to see if my plan would work."

"What plan?" asked Clara.

"You gave me the idea," said Beth. "We can't bring the gardens and fields to us, but we can go to the fields and gardens!"

"What do you mean?" asked Clara.

"Our existence relies on the flowers, trees, and plants that provide us with nectar and pollen. Some humans fail to recognize the importance of the work we do. But we know just how important we are. So I am going to move our whole colony. We will go to a place where there are plenty of gardens and fields that will provide for our needs," said Queen Beth.

Clara looked impressed, but she was also a little worried. "How are you going to do that?" she asked.

"Well, right now we have scouts searching for a good spot to build our new home. They will find a suitable and safe place for a new hive. Then they will come back to tell us which way to go. We will fly to the new location in a swarm. It will mean a lot of work, but it can be done if we all work together."

"With you in charge, I have no doubt that we will succeed," said Clara proudly.

Moments later the scouts returned, exhausted.

Chapter 4

The Swarm

The scouts took a much-needed rest. Then they did a special dance for the other bees in the hive. All the bees paid close attention to the dance. It was like a code, giving them directions to the spot where they would construct the new hive.

After filling up on whatever nectar they had available, the bees were ready to begin their journey.

"Let's go, everyone. Swarming will be hard work, but as soon as we get there, we will be able to start building our new home!" Queen Beth promised her colony.

The colony formed a swarm to make sure that all the bees were safe. Queen Beth was in the middle of the swarm. As they flew, they passed by fields that had been cleared in order to build houses.

"What a shame," said Clara. "It is because of barren fields like this that it is so hard for us to find a stable source of nectar and pollen."

After many hours of flying, Beth said, "I am growing tired. Let us rest for a while. We will need our strength to reach our new home." Not only was she tired from flying, but she was also sad after seeing those barren fields.

Chapter 5

A New Hive, a New Home

After resting for the night in a swarm on a nearby tree, the colony continued its journey. Not long after, the colony reached a large field that had flowers and plants as far as the eye could see.

"This is perfect. Just think of all the pollen!" exclaimed Beth. "You have all done a wonderful job. This is the perfect place for our new home."

"I have heard stories about this field, Your Majesty. It is maintained by a group of very thoughtful humans. They look after the plants, trees, and flowers because they know how important they are for us bees — and how important we are for their food!" Karina responded as she buzzed excitedly.

Their new home was in a tree hollow that overlooked the colorful field. Without wasting any time, the worker bees started to build the new hive as quickly as possible so that the colony would be safe.

As soon as the hive was ready, Beth took one final look around. She knew that once she entered this new hive, she would not come out again. She would be much too busy laying eggs.

As Beth happily buzzed around, Karina gently reminded her of her duties. "It is time to go into the hive, Your Majesty."

"I know, Karina. I just wanted one more moment to look around before I commit fully to my duties as queen. I am so grateful to have such a perfect environment for our hive."

Beth and Karina buzzed as they slowly made their way into the hive.

As Beth went into the hive, she looked around. Bees were busily going about their duties. Life as she knew it would continue. The hive was once again thriving and full of activity. It was good to be home.